ALGEBRA

THE STORY OF MATH
Core Principles of Mathematics

ALGEBRA

EDITED BY JASON TOBIN

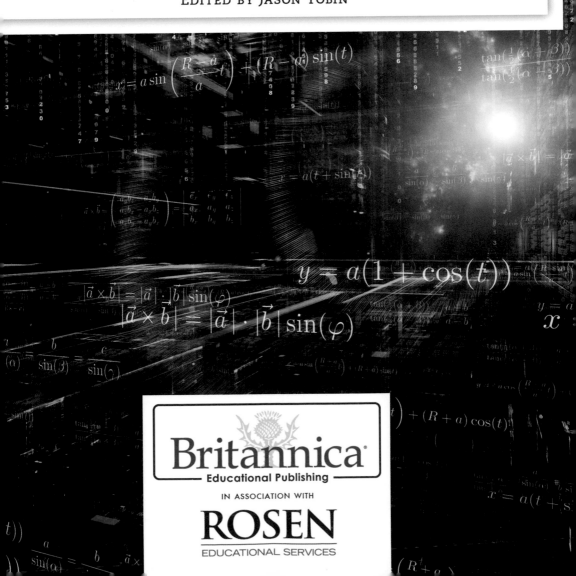

Britannica
Educational Publishing

IN ASSOCIATION WITH

ROSEN
EDUCATIONAL SERVICES

Published in 2015 by Britannica Educational Publishing (a trademark of Encyclopædia Britannica, Inc.) in association with The Rosen Publishing Group, Inc.
29 East 21st Street, New York, NY 10010

Distributed exclusively by Rosen Publishing.
To see additional Britannica Educational Publishing titles, go to rosenpublishing.com.

First Edition

Britannica Educational Publishing
J. E. Luebering: Director, Core Reference Group
Anthony L. Green: Editor, Compton's by Britannica

Rosen Publishing
Hope Lourie Killcoyne: Executive Editor
Jason Tobin: Editor
Nelson Sá: Art Director
Michael Moy: Designer
Cindy Reiman: Photography Manager
Karen Huang: Photo Researcher

Library of Congress Cataloging-in-Publication Data

Algebra/edited by Jason Tobin.—First edition.
    pages cm.—(The story of math: core principles of mathematics)
Audience: Grades 7 to 12.
Includes bibliographical references and index.
ISBN 978-1-62275-521-9 (library bound)
1. Algebra—Juvenile literature. I. Tobin, Jason (Jason Wesley), editor.
QA141.A44 2015
512—dc23

2014023206

Manufactured in the United States of America

Contents

Introduction

An important branch of mathematics, algebra is studied not only in high school and college, but in the lower grades as well. Although it is dreaded by many students, algebra can be an enjoyable subject. Algebra is practical and as useful as all the other branches of mathematics. For some careers, such as those in engineering and science, knowledge of algebra is indispensable. After reading these chapters, algebra will no longer seem intimidating. In fact, you may be surprised at how often you use it on a daily basis.

It is easy to get hung up on the symbols and complicated story problems for which algebra is famous. However, mathematical concepts that seem so mysterious are often used in regular conversation. The trick is learning how to translate math into English.

For example, suppose an 8-year-old boy asks his father how old he is. Instead of answering the boy directly, the father can attempt an experiment by replying that he is 30 years older than the boy. This is a problem that the son is interested in solving. He can quickly perform the addition and find that his father is 38 years old:

8 + 30 = 38

Suppose the boy then asks the age of his mother. The father might at this point present a more challenging problem. For example, the

Algebra is less difficult and more useful than many people think. Lisa F. Young/Shutterstock.com

father may answer that if the boy added six years to his mother's age, the result would be equal to the father's age. The father has thus found an excellent opportunity to help his son understand how an algebraic equation may be made up and solved.

The father writes the mother's age on a slip of paper and turns the slip over so the boy cannot see the numeral. He then lays the slip, blank side up, on a tablet. Next to the slip he writes the symbols that will help solve the problem:

$$\boxed{} + 6 = 38$$

The son takes only a moment to guess that his mother is 32 years old. When the father turns the slip of paper over, they see this answer is correct:

$$\boxed{32} + 6 = 38$$

This will have been the boy's first lesson in algebra because he essentially solved the equation $x + 6 = 38$.

The father did not say anything about a mysterious letter x that can stand for any number. Nor did he tell the boy about any rule such as "changing the sign of the six and writing it on the other side of the equation." Instead, the boy's first lesson in algebra evolved in a natural way from a problem in arithmetic.

When you study algebra in school, you will learn more about the relationship between algebra and arithmetic. Some of the fundamental concepts of algebra that are taught in school are explained in the following chapters. You will learn why algebra was developed; basic principles of algebra, such as variables, generalizations, and patterns; and everything you need to know about real numbers. More important, you will learn how to apply algebra's fundamental concepts. In no time at all, algebra will cease to be a mystery.

WHAT IS ALGEBRA?

Algebra has often been described as "arithmetic with letters." Unlike arithmetic, which deals with specific numbers, algebra introduces variables that greatly extend the generality and scope of arithmetic. This book will focus on the algebra taught in middle schools and high schools, often referred to as elementary algebra, which deals with the general properties of numbers and the relations between them.

ALGEBRAIC QUANTITIES

The principal distinguishing characteristic of algebra is the use of letters to represent numerical quantities and simple symbols to represent mathematical operations. Following a system that originated with the 17th-century French thinker René Descartes, letters, especially $x, y,$ and z, represent unknown quantities, or variables. The + and - signs indicate addition and subtraction of these quantities, but multiplication is simply indicated by adjacent letters. Thus, ax represents the product of a by x. This simple expression can be interpreted, for example, as the interest earned in one year by a sum of a dollars invested at an annual rate of x. It can also be interpreted as the distance traveled in a hours by a car moving at x miles per hour. Such flexibility of representation is what gives algebra its great utility.

THE BEGINNINGS OF ALGEBRA

More than 3,500 years ago an Egyptian named Ahmes collected a set of mathematical problems and their solutions. About 2,500 years ago the Greek mathematician Pythagoras started a religious-mathematical brotherhood. Intensely interested in geometry, they classified numbers according to geometrical properties. The famous Greek geometer

Euclid discovered important properties of numbers through a study of geometry.

Diophantus, another famous early Greek mathematician, has been called the father of algebra. He treated algebra from a purely numerical point of view. He made a special study of certain types of equations that are today called Diophantine equations.

Our modern word *algebra* comes from the Arabic *al-jabr*, which appeared in the title of an algebra text written in about 825 CE by the Arab astronomer and mathematician al-Khwarizmi. The word *algorithm* is derived from his name.

MODERN ALGEBRA

The study of the algebra of real numbers and the recent recognition of the fundamental importance of the basic principles have led to the development of what is now called modern algebra or abstract algebra.

The concepts of modern algebra have been found to be extremely useful in other branches of mathematics, as well as in the physical and social sciences. A chemist may use modern algebra in a study of the structure

DIOPHANTUS

Diophantus of Alexandria (*c.* 250 CE) was a Greek mathematician, famous for his work in algebra. One mathematical work he is believed to have written is a large and extremely influential treatise called *Arithmetica*.

(continued on the next page)

Pierre de Fermat extended the work of Diophantus by marking up a copy of the earlier mathematician's treatise Arithmetica. Courtesy of De Agostini Picture Library/Getty Images

(continued from the previous page)

Its historical importance is twofold: it is the first known work to employ algebra in a modern style, and it inspired the rebirth of number theory.

Although he had limited algebraic tools at his disposal, Diophantus managed to solve a great variety of problems, and *Arithmetica* inspired Arabic mathematicians such as al-Karajī (*c.* 980–1030) to apply his methods. The most famous extension of Diophantus's work was by Pierre de Fermat (1601–65), the founder of modern number theory. In the margins of his copy of *Arithmetica*, Fermat wrote various remarks proposing new solutions, corrections, and generalizations of Diophantus's methods as well as some conjectures, including what became known as Fermat's last theorem, which occupied mathematicians for generations to come. Indeterminate equations restricted to integral solutions have come to be known, though inappropriately, as Diophantine equations.

of crystals. An engineer may use modern algebra in designing a computer. A mathematician may use modern algebra in a study of logic.

Elementary algebra students study the properties of addition and multiplication of real numbers that follow as a consequence of certain basic principles. Students of modern algebra may work with any set of objects, not only with real numbers. Modern algebra considers certain operations on these objects that are not restricted to addition and subtraction as with elementary algebra. In modern algebra it is agreed that certain basic principles are satisfied by these operations, then various properties are derived from assumed basic principles. Modern or abstract algebra will not be discussed further in this book.

BASIC PRINCIPLES OF ALGEBRA

S ome of the fundamental concepts of algebra that are taught in school are explained
in this chapter. Their applications in solving
various types of mathematical problems are
discussed in chapter 4.

OPEN SENTENCES

Suppose that a class is asked to complete sentences to make true statements. For example:

1. ⬚ **is the capital of Pennsylvania.**
2. _____ **is the capital of California**
3. ⬚ **is the capital of Illinois.**

A student taking the test converted the first sentence into a true statement as follows:

1. ⟦ **Harrisburg** ⟧ is the capital of Pennsylvania.

He converted the second sentence into a false statement:

2. Hollywood is the capital of California.

He didn't know the name of the city that is the capital of Illinois, so he went on to the other sentences, leaving the third sentence open:

3. ⟮　　　　　　⟯ **is the capital of Illinois.**

By not filling in the blank in the third sentence, the student did not convert it into a true statement or into a false statement. Sentences that are neither true nor false are called open sentences. The problem of converting open sentences into true statements is quite common in mathematics.

VARIABLES

In mathematics, as in ordinary language, open sentences may be written without using blanks or frames. For example, the open sentence

$$\square + 3 = 5$$

may also be written $x + 3 = 5$. The open sentence $x + 3 = 5$ may be converted into a true statement or a false statement by replacing the mark x with a name. The x serves as a placeholder for a number. Other marks can also be used to serve as placeholders. Letters such as a, b, c, or x that are serving as placeholders are called variables.

The sentence $m + 3 = 8$ may be converted into a true statement by replacing the variable m with the numeral 5:

$$\textcircled{5} + 3 = 8 \quad \neq$$

In mathematics the multiplication sign × is often replaced by a dot •. Sometimes, as between a numeral and a variable, or between two variables, it is omitted altogether. Thus, for example, the sentence $3 \times a = 12$ may be written as $3 \cdot a = 12$ or $3a = 12$.

NUMERALS, EQUATIONS, AND SOLUTION SETS

The number of eggs in this carton

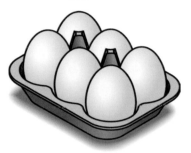

has many names. For example, 1/2 dozen, 6, $3 + 3$, 18/3, and $3 \cdot 2$ are all different names for the number of eggs in the carton.

A name for a number is called a numeral or a numerical expression. The open sentence $x - 4 = 2$ may be converted into a true statement by replacing x with any numeral that names the number of eggs in the carton pictured above. For example, the following are true statements:

$$6 - 4 = 2$$

$$(3 + 3) - 4 = 2, \text{ and}$$

$$(3 \cdot 3) - 4 = 2$$

Although the variable x may be replaced by many numerals to convert the open sentence $x-4=2$ into a true statement, all such numerals are names for the same number because there is one and only one number that satisfies this open sentence. It is true that the number 6 satisfies this open sentence, and that the number $3+3$ also satisfies this open sentence, but 6 and $3+3$ are just different names for the same number.

The sentence $6 - 4 = 2$ is called an equation. An equation tells you that the quantities on either side of the equal sign are the same. This equation tells us that $6-4$ is the same number as 2.

The equation $(3+3)-4=(3\bullet2)-4$ is a true statement because $(3+3)-4$ and $(3\bullet2)-4$ are names for the same number. On the left side of the equation, the parentheses in the numeral $(3+3)-4$ tell you that you may find another name for the number $(3+3)-4$ by first adding 3 and 3 and then subtracting 4 from their sum. On the right side of the equation, the parentheses in the numeral $(3\bullet2)-4$ tell you that you may find another name for the number $(3\bullet2)-4$ by first multiplying 3 by 2 and then subtracting 4 from their product.

The open sentence $x-4=2$ is also called an equation. The set of all numbers that satisfy this equation is called the solution set of the equation. The solution set of this equation consists of just the number 6 because 6 is the only number that satisfies this equation.

A shorthand notation for the set of all numbers that satisfy the equation $x-4=2$ is $\{x:x-4=2\}$. We may read this as "the set of all numbers x such that $x-4=2$."

The sentence $\{x:x-4=2\}=\{6\}$ says that the set of all numbers that satisfy the equation $x-4=2$ consists of just the number 6.

Sometimes, solution sets consist of several numbers because there are several numbers that can satisfy an equation. For example, when any number is multiplied by 0, the result is 0. Thus, the solution set of the equation $x\bullet 0=0$ consists of every number: $\{x:x\bullet 0=0\}$ consists of all numbers.

GENERALIZATIONS

When we say, for example, that there exists a number *x* with such a property that $x-5=3$, it is called a generalization. Since we are saying that there exists among the numbers one that has a certain property, the sentence is called an existential generalization. Existential generalizations are often written in an abbreviated form by using a turned-around E. The sentence $\exists_x x - 4 = 2$ is a shorthand notation that tells you that there exists a number with such a property that when 4 is subtracted from it the result is 2.

Recall that each number has such a property that when it is multiplied by 0 the result is 0. More briefly, we may say that for each number x, $x \cdot 0 = 0$. This last sentence tells us about a property of numbers, and it too is called a generalization. Since it tells us that each number has a certain property, the sentence is called a universal generalization. Universal generalizations are often written in an abbreviated form by using an upside-down A.

The sentence $\forall_x x \cdot 0 = 0$ is a shorthand notation that tells you that each number has such a property that when it is multiplied by 0, the result is 0.

PATTERNS AND PRINCIPLES

Now comes a very important fundamental property of numbers. Notice that, for each pair of numbers, the result of adding the second number to the first is the same as that for

ÉVARISTE GALOIS

Évariste Galois (1811-32) was a French mathematician famous for his contributions to the part of higher algebra now known as group theory. His theory provided a solution to the long-standing question of determining when an algebraic equation can be solved by radicals.

The circumstances that led to Galois's death in a duel in Paris are not altogether clear, but recent scholarship suggests that it was at his own insistence that the duel was staged and fought to look like a police ambush. In any case, anticipating his death the night before the duel, Galois hastily wrote a scientific last testament addressed to his

Évariste Galois. Courtesy of the Bibliothèque Nationale, Paris

(continued on the next page)

friend Auguste Chevalier in which he summarized his work and included some new theorems and conjectures.

Galois's manuscripts were published in 1846. But it was not until 1870, with the publication of Camille Jordan's *Traité des Substitutions*, that group theory became a fully established part of mathematics.

adding the first number to the second. For example:

$$\boxed{2} + \textbf{\textcircled{3}} = \textbf{\textcircled{3}} + \boxed{2} \quad \begin{cases} 2 + 3 = 5 \\ 3 + 2 = 5 \end{cases}$$

$$\boxed{5} + \textbf{\textcircled{15}} = \textbf{\textcircled{15}} + \boxed{5} \quad \begin{cases} 5 + 15 = 20 \\ 15 + 5 = 20 \end{cases}$$

Because of this property, each pair of numbers satisfies the open sentence $x+y=y+x$. We agree that each occurrence of the variable x is to be replaced by a first numeral and that each occurrence of the variable y is to be replaced by a second numeral.

The property of numbers to which we have been referring may be stated as follows:

$$V_x V_y \, x+y=y+x$$

This universal generalization is called the commutative principle for addition. It tells you that for each x and each y, $x+y=y+x$. This is a true generalization because all of its instances are true statements.

The universal generalization

$$V_{x \neq 0} \; x \bullet 1/x = 1$$

tells you that each nonzero number satisfies the open sentence

$$\boxed{} \bullet \dfrac{1}{\boxed{}} \; = \; 1$$

This generalization is also a true statement because all of its instances are true statements. For example, the following instances are true statements:

$$\boxed{2} \bullet \dfrac{1}{\boxed{2}} = 1 \qquad \boxed{4} \bullet \dfrac{1}{\boxed{4}} = 1$$

The first of these sentences tells you, for example, that two halves of a pie is one pie.

The second sentence tells you, for example, that four quarters of a pie is one pie. The number 1/2 is called the reciprocal of 2; the number 1/4 is the reciprocal of 4.

Another basic property of numbers is suggested by the multiplication tables. For example, consider the following:

$$
\begin{array}{rcl}
1 \cdot 2 &=& 2 \\
2 \cdot 2 &=& 4 \\
3 \cdot 2 &=& 6 \\
4 \cdot 2 &=& 8 \\
5 \cdot 2 &=& 10 \\
6 \cdot 2 &=& 12 \\
7 \cdot 2 &=& 14
\end{array}
$$

$$3 + 4 = 7 \qquad\qquad 6 + 8 = 14$$

We see that the following sentence is a true statement:

$$\left(\diamond_3 + \blacktriangle_4 \right) \cdot \boxed{2} = \left(\diamond_3 \cdot \boxed{2} \right) + \left(\blacktriangle_4 \cdot \boxed{2} \right)$$

The open sentence

$$\left(\diamond + \blacktriangle\right)\cdot\square = \left(\diamond\cdot\square\right) + \left(\blacktriangle\cdot\square\right)$$

is converted into a true statement if a first numeral is written in each diamond-shaped frame, a second numeral is written in each triangular frame, and a third numeral is written in each square frame.

The universal generalization $V_x V_y V_z$ $(x+y)\bullet z = (x\bullet z)+(y\bullet z)$ tells you that for each x, each y, and each z, the result of multiplying the sum of x and y by z is the same as the result obtained by multiplying x by z and y by z and then adding the products.

This universal generalization is called the distributive principle. It is a true generalization because all of its instances are true. Thus, for example, the complicated numerical expression $(27\bullet 18)+(73\bullet 18)$ may be simplified quite easily by noticing that, by the distributive principle, as follows:

$$\left(\diamondsuit{\scriptstyle27} \cdot \boxed{18} \right) + \left(\blacktriangle{\scriptstyle73} \cdot \boxed{18} \right) = \left(\diamondsuit{\scriptstyle27} + \blacktriangle{\scriptstyle73} \right) \cdot \boxed{18}$$

$$= 100 \cdot \boxed{18}$$
$$= 1800$$

$$\text{So, } (27 \cdot 18) + (73 \cdot 18) = 1800$$

REAL NUMBERS

Real numbers are numbers that are used as measures of directed change—they measure direction as well as magnitude. For example, if you gain 10 pounds, the change in your weight is measured by the real number +10 ["positive ten"]. If you go on a diet and lose 10 pounds, the change in your weight is measured by the real number −10 ["negative ten"].

The set of real numbers consists of all the positive numbers, all the negative numbers, and 0. Corresponding to each nonzero number-of-arithmetic there are exactly two real numbers: one positive number and one negative number.

The sum of a pair of real numbers is the real number that is the measure of the result of the directed changes. For example, if you gain 10 pounds [a change in weight measured by the real number +10] and then lose 6 pounds [a change in weight measured by −6], the resultant change in weight is a gain of 4 pounds [measured by +4]. For short, +10 + −6 = +4.

We say that the opposite of +10 is −10 and that the opposite of −10 is +10. The opposite of a given real number is called the additive inverse. For each real number the sum of that real number and its opposite is 0.

BASIC PRINCIPLES
FOR ADDITION

There are certain principles concerning addition of real numbers. These are called basic principles. First there are the three principles mentioned above:

(AO) $\Bigg\{$

(A) THE SUM OF A PAIR OF REAL NUMBERS IS A REAL NUMBER.

(B) 0 IS A REAL NUMBER.

(C) THE OPPOSITE OF A REAL NUMBER IS A REAL NUMBER.

Notice that a gain of 10 pounds followed by a loss of 6 pounds, $+10 + -6$, results in the same change in weight as a loss of 6 pounds followed by a gain of 10 pounds, $-6 + +10$, Thus,

$$\boxed{+10} \; + \; \bullet\text{-6}\bullet \; = \; \bullet\text{-6}\bullet \; + \; \boxed{+10}$$

This suggests that addition of real numbers is a commutative operation, and we accept this as another of our basic principles for addition of real numbers:

(A1) $V_x \, V_y \; x + y = y + x$

A gain of 10 pounds followed by no further gain or loss of weight results in a gain of 10 pounds:

$$\boxed{+10} \; + \; 0 \; = \; \boxed{+10}$$

This suggests our next basic principle:

(A2) $V_x \; x + 0 = x$

We mentioned in the last section that the sum of a real number and its opposite is 0. We accept this as another basic principle:

(A3) $V_x \; x + -x = 0$

Finally we complete our list of basic principles with the associative principle for addition of real numbers. Before stating this principle, let us consider an example.

Suppose that you go on a two-week vacation. If you gain 2 pounds the first week and lose 3 pounds the second week [a resultant change in weight measured by the real number +2 +−3] and then come home and gain 4 pounds [+4], your resultant change in weight is measured by the real number (+2 +−3) + +4. If, instead, you gained 2 pounds [+2] the week before going on vacation and then lost 3 pounds the first week and gained 4 pounds the second week [−3 + +4] of vacation, your resultant change in weight is measured by the real number

$$^+2 + (^-3 + {}^+4)$$

Since $(^+2 + {}^-3) + {}^+4 = {}^-1 + {}^+4 = {}^+3$

and $^+2 + (^-3 + {}^+4) = {}^+2 + {}^+1 = {}^+3,$

it follows that

$$\left(\boxed{{}^+2} + \triangle_3\right) + \left({}^+4\right) = \boxed{{}^+2} + \left(\triangle_3 + \left({}^+4\right)\right)$$

This suggests that the open sentence

$$\left(\square + \triangle\right) + \bigcirc = \square + \left(\triangle + \bigcirc\right)$$

is converted into a true statement if a first numeral is written in each square frame, a second numeral is written in each diamond-shaped frame, and a third numeral is written in each circular frame.

The universal generalization

(A4) $V_x \ V_y \ V_z \ (x+y)+z = x+(y+z)$

is called the associative principle for addition of real numbers. This basic principle tells you that for each x, each y, and each z, the result of adding $(x+y)$ and z is the same as the result of adding x and $(y+z)$.

A short way of saying that addition of real numbers satisfies the basic principles (A0) through (A4) is to say that the set of real numbers is a commutative group under addition.

BASIC PRINCIPLES OF MULTIPLICATION

Consideration of real numbers as measures of directed change suggests basic principles for multiplication of real numbers.

If a given real number is multiplied by the real number +1, the product is the given real number. For example:

$$\boxed{^+2} \cdot {}^+1 = \boxed{^+2} \qquad\qquad \boxed{^-2} \cdot {}^+1 = \boxed{^-2}$$

Each real number [except 0] has a multiplicative inverse, called the reciprocal. The result of multiplying a real number by its reciprocal is +1.

Multiplication of real numbers also satisfies the commutative principle and the associative principle. These investigations of properties of real numbers suggest a list of basic principles for multiplication of real numbers that are similar to the basic principles for addition of real numbers. Corresponding to the basic principle (A0), we accept the basic principle:

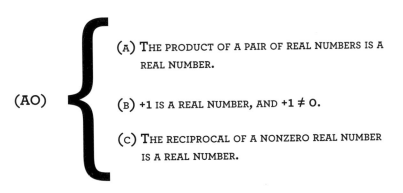

(A0)

(A) THE PRODUCT OF A PAIR OF REAL NUMBERS IS A REAL NUMBER.

(B) +1 IS A REAL NUMBER, AND +1 ≠ 0.

(C) THE RECIPROCAL OF A NONZERO REAL NUMBER IS A REAL NUMBER.

Corresponding to the basic principles (A1) through (A4), we accept the basic principles:

$$(M1) \quad \bigvee_{x} \bigvee_{y} x \bullet y = y \bullet x$$

$$(M2) \quad \bigvee_{x} x \bullet +1 = x$$

$$(M3) \quad \bigvee_{x \neq 0} x \bullet +1/x = +1$$

$$(M4) \quad \bigvee_{x} \bigvee_{y} \bigvee_{z} (x \bullet y) \bullet z = x \bullet (y \bullet z)$$

The basic principle (M3) tells you that the product of each nonzero real number $(\bigvee_{x \neq 0})$ and its reciprocal is +1.

Finally we complete our list of basic principles for addition and multiplication of real

AL-KHWARIZMI

The Arab mathematician al-Khwarizmi was born in Baghdad, Iraq, in about 780. His full name was Muhammad ibn Musa al-Khwarizmi. He compiled a set of astronomical tables and wrote a treatise, *Kitab al-jabr wa al-muqabalah* (The Book of Integration and Equation), from which the term *algebra* was derived. He is also known for a work that introduced Arabic numerals and methods of calculation by decimal notation to the Western world. The word *algorithm* originated from the Latin title of that work, *Al-goritmi de numero Indorum.*

Al-Khwarizmi. Sovfoto/Universal Images Group/Getty Images

numbers by adding the distributive principle to the list:

$$(D_1) \quad V_x \; V_y \; V_z \; (x+y) \bullet z = (x \bullet z) + (y \bullet z)$$

The next section will feature examples of how these principles can be used to deduce other properties of addition and multiplication of real numbers.

USING REAL NUMBERS

An example of the use of real numbers is in the measurement of temperatures. If it is a very cold day, it may not be enough to tell someone that the temperature is 5 degrees; you may have to indicate whether it is 5 degrees above zero or 5 degrees below zero. You may use the real numbers +5 or −5 to indicate the temperature.

It may be helpful to picture the set of real numbers as the set of points on a line:

A diagram such as this is often called a picture of the number line. The point labeled 0 is called the origin. The number-of-arithmetic 5 is the arithmetic value of the real numbers +5 and −5. The numbers-of-arithmetic are used as measures of magnitude; the real numbers are used as measures of magnitude and direction.

OPERATIONS ON REAL NUMBERS

As previously mentioned, the sum of a pair of real numbers is the real number that is the measure of the resultant of the corresponding pair of directed changes. To gain further insight into addition of real numbers it may be convenient to refer to a picture of the number line.

For example:

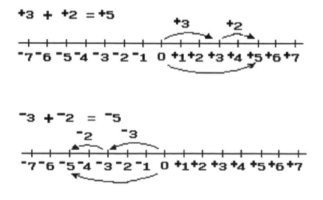

Notice that we may apply our knowledge of addition of numbers-of-arithmetic when we wish to add a pair of positive numbers [or a pair of negative numbers]; for the arithmetic value of the sum of a pair of positive numbers [or of a pair of negative numbers] is the sum of their arithmetic values: 3 + 2 = 5.

To find the sum of a positive number and a negative number, for example:

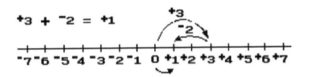

or the sum of a negative number and a positive number, for example:

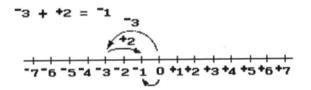

we may apply our knowledge of subtraction of numbers-of-arithmetic: 3−2=1.

Multiplication of real numbers is similarly related to multiplication of numbers-of-arithmetic:

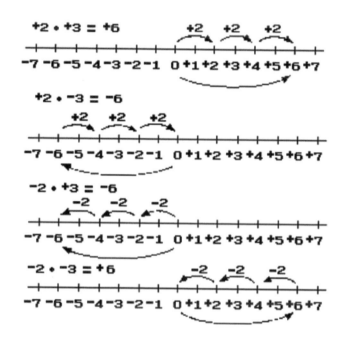

The arithmetic value of the product of a pair of real numbers is the product of their arithmetic values: $2 \cdot 3 = 6$. The product of a positive number by a positive number [or of a negative number by a negative number] is a positive number. The product of a positive number by a negative number [or of a negative number by a positive number] is a negative number.

Let us see what it means to divide +6 by +3. We wish to find the real number that satisfies the open sentence

$$^+6 \cdot \frac{^+1}{^+3} = \square$$

A real number satisfies this open sentence if and only if it satisfies the following open sentence:

$$\left(^+6 \cdot \frac{^+1}{^+3}\right) \cdot {}^+3 = \square \cdot {}^+3$$

But,
$$\left(^+6 \cdot \frac{^+1}{^+3}\right) \cdot {}^+3 = {}^+6 \cdot \left(\frac{^+1}{^+3} \cdot {}^+3\right)$$

$$= {}^+6 \cdot \left({}^+3 \cdot \frac{^+1}{^+3}\right)$$

$$= {}^+6 \cdot {}^+1$$

$$= \underline{{}^+6}$$

So a real number satisfies the open sentence

$$^+6 \cdot \frac{^+1}{^+3} = \square$$

if and only if it satisfies the open sentence

$$\underline{^+6} = \square \cdot {}^+3$$

We notice that +2 is the real number that satisfies the last open sentence

$$\underline{^+6} = \boxed{^+2} \cdot {}^+3$$

So it follows that

$$^+6 \cdot \frac{^+1}{^+3} = \boxed{^+2}$$

or, equivalently, that

$$^+6 \div {}^+3 = \boxed{^+2}$$

APPLYING THE FUNDAMENTAL CONCEPTS OF ALGEBRA

An understanding of the fundamental concepts of algebra and of how those fundamental concepts may be applied is necessary in many professional and most technical careers. For engineers and scientists it is an essential requirement.

Now that you understand the fundamental concepts of algebra, let's examine how these concepts may be applied to aid in the solution of various types of mathematical problems.

FORMULAS, FUNCTIONS, AND GRAPHS

A fruit dealer sells apples priced at 12 cents each. He may find it convenient to make a list of the cost of various quantities of apples:

Number of apples	Cost
0	$0
1	.12
2	.24
3	.36

To find the cost of any quantity of apples he may use the formula $C = .12 \cdot N$. If he substitutes a numeral for N, he can find the corresponding cost by using this formula. For example, to find the cost of 17 apples he substitutes 17 for N: $C = .12 \cdot 17$. If he multiplies .12 by 17, he finds that the cost of 17 apples is $2.04.

If the values of N are the whole numbers 0, 1, 2, 3,..., then the values of C are simply the multiples of .12.

It is also useful to consider the set of ordered pairs: $\{(0,0), (1, .12), (2, .24),...\}$

The first member of an ordered pair is called the first component, and the second member of an ordered pair is called the second component. Notice that in the set of ordered pairs that we are considering, no two ordered pairs have the same first component. This is called a function.

The domain of a function is the set of first components of the set of ordered pairs of which the function consists. The range of a function is the set of second components. In the example considered above, the domain of the function is the set of whole numbers, and the range of the function is the set of multiples of .12.

Instead of listing the costs of various quantities of apples, the dealer may make a graph:

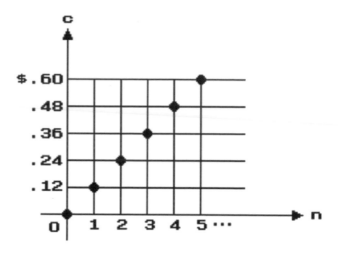

The dot that is above 1 and to the right of .12 illustrates the point that corresponds to the ordered pair (1, .12). The dot that is above 2 and to the right of .24 illustrates the point corresponding to the ordered pair (2, .24). By referring to the graph, the dealer can see at a glance that the cost of 4 apples is 48 cents.

LINEAR FUNCTIONS

Consider the set of all ordered pairs of real numbers (x, y) that satisfy the condition that the sum of the first and second components is +5; that is, x+y=+5. Some ordered pairs that belong to this function are: (+5, 0), (3 1/2, 1 1/2), (+6, −1).

This set of ordered pairs may also be described as the set of all ordered pairs of real numbers (x, y) such that y=⁻1•x++5. This set of ordered pairs of real numbers is a function whose domain and range is the set of all real numbers. The graph of this function is a line:

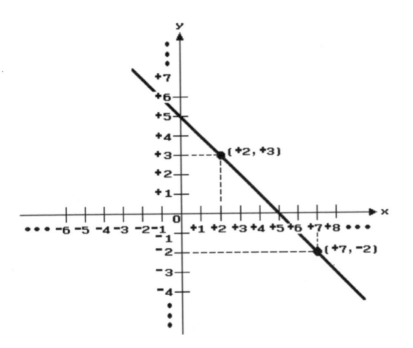

The points on the graph that correspond to the ordered pairs (+2, +3) and (+7, −2) are marked on the graph. You may find it worthwhile to locate the points on the graph that correspond to the following ordered pairs: (0, +5), (+1.5, +3.5), (−1, +6).

Since the graph of the function is a line, the function is called a linear function, and the equation y = −1 • x + +5 is called a linear equation.

BOOLEAN ALGEBRA

An important branch of mathematics is called Boolean algebra, named for the English mathematician and logician George Boole (1815–64). It combines algebraic methods and logic. The basic principles of Boolean algebra are very much like those of the algebra of real numbers. Boolean algebra is of significance to the theory of probability, geometry of sets, and information theory. A knowledge of Boolean algebra is very useful in such fields as computer programming and electronic-circuit construction, which require the application of mathematics and logic.

George Boole. Courtesy of the trustees of the British Museum; photograph, J.R. Freeman & Co. Ltd.

QUADRATIC FUNCTIONS

When we multiply a real number by itself, we can shorten the notation from n • n to n^2 ("n squared"). The numeral 2 is called an exponent.

The set of all ordered pairs of real numbers (x, y) such that $y = x^2$ is a function. Some ordered pairs that belong to this function are: (0,0) (+1, +1), (−1, +1), (+2, +4), (−2, +4).

The graph of this function is a parabola; the function is a quadratic function:

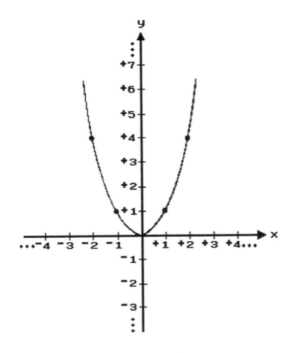

PROPERTIES OF
EXPONENTS

From the basic principles for addition and multiplication of real numbers, other principles
were derived. We now note some properties
of exponents that follow easily from the basic
principles.

For example,

$2^2 \cdot 2^3 = (2 \cdot 2) \cdot (2 \cdot 2 \cdot 2)$

$= 4 \cdot 8$

$= 32$

and $2^5 = 2 \cdot 2 \cdot 2 \cdot 2 \cdot 2 = 32$.

In fact, it is easy to prove the following
principle: $\bigvee_x x^2 \cdot x^3 = x^5$. This principle tells you
that for each real number x, the product of x^2
by x^3 is x^5. [Notice that $2 + 3 = 5$.]

Note also, for example, that

$$\frac{2^5}{2^2} = \frac{2 \cdot 2 \cdot 2 \cdot 2 \cdot 2}{2 \cdot 2} = \frac{32}{4} = 8 = 2 \cdot 2 \cdot 2 = 2^3$$

and that $\dfrac{2^2}{2^5} = \dfrac{2 \cdot 2}{2 \cdot 2 \cdot 2 \cdot 2 \cdot 2} = \dfrac{4}{32} = \dfrac{1}{8} = \dfrac{1}{2 \cdot 2 \cdot 2} = \dfrac{1}{2^3}$

These examples suggest the following principles that are easily proved to be consequences
of the basic principles:

$$\forall_{x \neq 0} \ \frac{x^5}{x^2} = x^3 \qquad \forall_{x \neq 0} \ \frac{x^2}{x^5} = \frac{1}{x^3}$$

[Notice that $5 - 2 = 3$.]

PRODUCTS AND FACTORING

You already know that for each real number a, $2 \bullet a + 3 \bullet a = 5 \bullet a$. This follows from the distributive principle.

Consider now the indicated product: $(a + 2) \bullet (a + 3)$. From the basic principles it follows that:

$$(a + 2) \bullet (a + 3) = (a + 2) \bullet a + (a + 2) \bullet 3$$
$$= (a^2 + 2 \bullet a) + (a \bullet 3 + 2 \bullet 3) =$$
$$(a^2 + 2 \bullet a) + (3 \bullet a + 6) =$$
$$a^2 + (2 \bullet a + 3 \bullet a) + 6$$
$$= a^2 + 5 \bullet a + 6$$

Thus,

$$(a + 2) \bullet (a + 3) = a^2 + 5 \bullet a + 6$$

We say that the expression $a^2 + 5 \bullet a + 6$ is the expanded form of the indicated product $(a + 2) \bullet (a + 3)$.

When we transform an expression into an indicated product, we say that the expression has been factored. We see that the expression $a^2 + 5 \cdot a + 6$ may be factored, and that its factors are $(a + 2)$ and $(a + 3)$.

Notice that for each pair of real numbers a and b:

$$(a+b) \cdot (a+b) = (a+b) \cdot a + (a+b) \cdot b$$
$$= (a^2 + b \cdot a) + (a \cdot b + b^2)$$
$$= a^2 + (a \cdot b + a \cdot b) + b^2$$
$$= a^2 + 2 \cdot a \cdot b + b^2$$

Thus,

$$(a+b) \cdot (a+b) = a^2 + 2 \cdot a \cdot b + b^2$$

and we see that for each pair of real numbers a and b, the expression $a^2 + 2 \cdot a \cdot b + b^2$ may be factored.

For each pair of real numbers a and b, the expression $a^2 - b^2$ may also be factored. This is demonstrated as follows:

$$(a-b) \cdot (a+b) = (a-b) \cdot a + (a-b) \cdot b$$
$$= (a^2 - b \cdot a) + (a \cdot b - b^2)$$
$$= (a^2 + -a \cdot b) + (a \cdot b - b^2)$$
$$= a^2 + (-a \cdot b + a \cdot b) - b^2$$
$$= a^2 + 0 - b^2$$
$$= a^2 - b^2$$

Thus,

$$(a-b) \cdot (a+b) = a^2 - b^2$$

The ability to factor is also important in finding the solutions of quadratic equations.

QUADRATIC EQUATIONS

Consider the equation $x^2 - +25 = 0$. This equation is an example of a quadratic equation. The real numbers +5 and −5 both satisfy the above open sentence:

$$\boxed{+5}^2 - {}^+25 = 0$$

$$\boxed{-5}^2 - {}^+25 = 0$$

The solution set of the given equation consists of simply the real numbers +5 and −5. We say that +5 and −5 are the two roots of the given quadratic equation.

When we are trying to find the roots of a quadratic equation, we often make use of an important principle of real numbers. This principle states that the product of a pair of real numbers is 0 if and only if one of the numbers is 0. That is, $V_x V_y \, xy = 0$ if and only if $x = 0$ or $y = 0$.

Let us see how we may use this principle to find the roots of the quadratic equation $x^2 - +16 = 0$. We first notice that the expression $x^2 - +16$ may be factored:

$$x^2 - +16 = x^2 - +4^2 = (x - +4) \cdot (x + +4)$$

Thus, we may transform the given equation $x^2 - +16 = 0$ into the equivalent equation $(x - +4) \cdot (x + +4) = 0$. A real number satisfies the last equation if and only if it satisfies the given equation.

We know that $(x - +4) \cdot (x + +4) = 0$ if and only if $x - +4 = 0$ or $x + +4 = 0$. Thus, a real number satisfies the equation $(x - +4) \cdot (x + +4) = 0$ if and only if the real number satisfies one of the following equations: $x - +4 = 0$ or $x + +4 = 0$. The solution set of the equation $x - +4 = 0$ consists of simply the number +4 since

$$\boxed{+4} - {}^+4 = 0$$

The solution set of the equation $x + +4 = 0$ consists of simply the number −4, since

$$\boxed{-4} + {}^+4 = 0$$

Thus, the solution set of the equation $(x - +4) \cdot (x + +4) = 0$ consists of the numbers +4 and −4. Hence the roots of the given quadratic equation $x^2 - +16 = 0$ are the numbers +4 and −4. We may check this result:

$$\boxed{^+4}^2 - \,^+16 = 0 \quad \text{and} \quad \boxed{^-4}^2 - \,^+16 = 0$$

SOLVING PROBLEMS

The following are some typical problems that, in a natural way, lead us to algebraic equations. In each problem, the solution to the problem is found by finding the solution set of an equation. When we find the solution set of an equation, we say that we have solved the equation.

Example 1: A number has such a property that when 6 is subtracted from twice the number, the result is 16. What is the number?

Solution: The required number must satisfy the open sentence

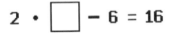

$$2 \cdot \boxed{} - 6 = 16$$

or, equivalently, the required number must satisfy each of the following open sentences:

$$(2 \cdot \boxed{} - 6) + 6 = 16 + 6$$

$$2 \cdot \boxed{} = 22$$

$$\tfrac{1}{2}(2 \cdot \boxed{}) = \tfrac{1}{2} \cdot 22$$

$$\boxed{} = 11$$

Since the only number that satisfies the last equation is 11, 11 is the required number. We may check our result:

Check:

$$2 \cdot \boxed{11} - 6 = 22 - 6 = 16$$

Example 2: A number has such a property that when 10 is subtracted from twice the number, the result is the same as when 6 is added to the number. What is the number?

Solution: A number has the required property if and only if it satisfies the open sentence $2 \cdot x - 10 = x + 6$ or, equivalently, a number has the required property if and only if it satisfies each of the following open sentences:

$$(2 \cdot x - 10) + 10 = (x + 6) + 10$$
$$2x = x + 16$$
$$-x + 2x = -x + (x + 16)$$
$$(-x + x) + x = (-x + x) + 16$$
$$x = 16$$

The only number that satisfies the last open sentence is 16. Therefore, 16 is the required number.

Check:

$$2 \cdot \boxed{16} - 10 = \boxed{16} + 6$$

Example 3: Suppose that Tom has $6.00 more than Bill and that together they have a total of $12.00. How much money does Tom have? How much money does Bill have?

Solution: Suppose that Tom has t dollars and that Bill has b dollars. Since Tom has $6.00 more than Bill, then

(1) $t = 6 + b$

Since Tom and Bill have together a total of $12.00, then

(2) $t + b = 12$

Equation (1) tells us that t is the same as $6 + b$. We may therefore replace t with $6 + b$ in equation (2):

$(6 + b) + b = 12.$

Thus,

$6 + 2b = 12$

$2b = 6$

$b = 3$

Therefore Bill has $3.00. It follows that

$t = 6 + b = 6 + 3 = 9$

and so Tom has $9.00.

Check:

(1) $9 = 6 + 3$

(2) $9 + 3 = 12$

Conclusion

Now that you have learned the basics of algebra, can you see how it is useful for many applications in everyday life? It should not be difficult to imagine the many jobs that rely on an understanding of algebra.

Algebra is fundamental not only to all further mathematics and statistics but to the natural sciences, computer science, economics, and business. Along with writing, it is a cornerstone of modern scientific and technological civilization. Its roots can be traced all the way back to ancient civilizations.

Let's review the primary topics of algebra, specifically elementary algebra, the branch taught in middle and high school:

- Real and complex numbers, constants, and variables—collectively known as algebraic quantities.
- Rules of operation for such quantities.
- Geometric representations of such quantities.
- Formation of expressions involving algebraic quantities.
- Rules for manipulating such expressions.
- Formation of sentences, also called equations, involving algebraic expressions.

- Solution of equations and systems of equations.

Now that you've learned the language of algebra, you have a foundation upon which to build even more mathematical knowledge.

additive inverse The opposite of a given real number.

algebra A branch of mathematics that uses letters to represent numbers and that studies numbers and the operations (as multiplication and addition) that are used on them.

associative principle Universal generalization that produces the same mathematical value no matter how an expression's elements are grouped.

Boolean algebra Branch of mathematics that combines algebraic methods and logic.

commutative principle Universal generalization that states that a given operation and set will have the same results when the order of the two elements of the set is different.

distributive principle Universal generalization of obtaining the same mathematical result when an operation is carried out on a whole expression and when it is carried out on each part of an expression with the results then collected together.

domain The set of first components of the set of ordered pairs of which a function consists.

equation A statement of the equality of two mathematical expressions.

existential generalization A generalization that says there exists among the numbers one that has a certain property, abbreviated by ∃.

exponent A symbol written above and to the right of a mathematical expression to mean raising that expression to the power of the symbol.

function A mathematical relationship that assigns exactly one element of one set to each element of the same or another set.

generalization A general statement, law, principle, or proposition.

linear equation An equation in which each term is either a constant or contains only one variable, in which each variable has an exponent of 1, and which always has a straight line as a graph.

linear function A function whose graph is a nonvertical straight line.

notation A system of marks, signs, figures, or characters used to give specified information.

numeral A name for a number.

open sentence A sentence that is neither true nor false.

ordered pair A set of two numbers, or components, that can be used to plot a point on a graph.

quadratic equation An equation containing one term in which the unknown is squared and no term in which it is raised to a power higher than 2.

quadratic function A function whose graph is a parabola.

range The set of second components of the set of ordered pairs of which a function consists.

real number Any of the rational and irrational numbers.

reciprocal The multiplicative inverse of a real number.

solution The answer to a problem.

solution set The set of all numbers that satisfy an equation.

universal generalization A generalization that states that each number has a certain property, abbreviated by V.

variable Letter that serves as a placeholder.

The Algebra Project
99 Bishop Allen Drive
Cambridge, MA 02139
(617) 491-0200
Website: http://www.algebra.org
The Algebra Project is a national nonprofit
organization that uses mathematics as an
organizing tool to ensure a quality public
school education for every child in America.
The organization believes that every child
has a right to a quality education to succeed
in our technology-based society and to exer-
cise full citizenship.

American Mathematical Society (AMS)
201 Charles Street
Providence, RI 02904-2294
(800) 321-4267
Website: http://www.ams.org
The AMS serves the national and international
community through its publications, meet-
ings, advocacy, and other programs. Students
at all levels can benefit from AMS programs
and services. In addition to offering an
array of programs and opportunities for students, the AMS collects information about
opportunities of interest to students in the
mathematical sciences.

Canada/USA Mathcamp
129 Hancock Street
Cambridge, MA 02139
(888) 371-4159
Website: http://www.mathcamp.org
Canada/USA Mathcamp is an intensive
five-week-long summer program for math-
ematically talented high school students,
designed to expose these students to the
beauty of advanced mathematical ideas and
to new ways of thinking. More than just a
summer camp, Mathcamp is a vibrant community, made up of a wide variety of people
who share a common love of learning and
passion for mathematics.

Canadian Mathematical Society (CMS)
209 - 1725 St. Laurent Boulevard
Ottawa ON K1G 3V4
Canada
(613) 733-2662 x785
Website: https://cms.math.ca/Community/
Canada
The focus of the CMS is to form new part-
nerships with the users of mathematics
in business, governments, and universi-
ties, as well as educators in the school and
college systems and other mathematical

associations; and in doing so, share experiences, work on collaborative projects, and generally enhance the perception and strengthen the profile of mathematics in Canada.

Mathematical Association of America
1529 18th Street NW
Washington, DC 20036-1358
(800) 741-9415
Website: http://www.maa.org
The Mathematical Association of America is the largest professional society that focuses on mathematics accessible at the undergraduate level. Members include university, college, and high school teachers; graduate and undergraduate students; pure and applied mathematicians; computer scientists; statisticians; and many others in academia, government, business, and industry.

Technology Student Association (TSA)
1914 Association Drive
Reston, VA 20191-1540
(703) 860-9000
Website: http://www.tsaweb.org
The Technology Student Association is the only student organization devoted exclusively to

the needs of students engaged in science, technology, engineering, and mathematics (STEM). TSA's membership includes over 200,000 middle and high school students in over 2,000 schools spanning 49 states. Members learn through competitive events, leadership opportunities, and much more.

WEBSITES

Because of the changing nature of Internet links, Rosen Publishing has developed an online list of websites related to the subject of this book. This site is updated regularly. Please use this link to access this list:

http://www.rosenlinks.com/TSOM/Alg

For Further Reading

Brezina, Corona. *Al-Khwarizmi*. New York, NY: Rosen Publishing, 2005.

Downing, Douglas. *E-Z Algebra*. Hauppauge, NY: Barron's Educational Services, 2009.

Hasan, Heather. *Archimedes*. New York, NY: Rosen Publishing, 2006.

Huettenmueller, Rhonda. *Algebra Demystified*. New York: McGraw-Hill Professional, 2011.

Johnson, Mildred. *How to Solve Word Problems in Algebra*. New York: McGraw-Hill, 2000.

Kelley, Michael W. *The Humongous Book of Algebra Problems*. New York, NY: Penguin, 2008.

Long, Lynette. *Painless Algebra*. Hauppauge, NY: Barron's Educational Series, 2011.

McKellar, Danica. *Hot X: Algebra Exposed!* New York, NY: Penguin, 2010.

McMillan, Dawn. *Learning Algebra with Pizza*. North Mankato, MN: Capstone Press, 2011.

Rappaport, Josh, and Sally Blakemore. *Algebra Survival Guide*. Santa Fe, NM: Singing Turtle Press, 2000.

Selby, Peter H. *Practical Algebra: A Self-Teaching Guide*. Hoboken, NJ: Wiley, 1991.

Sterling, Mary Jane. *Algebra I for Dummies*. Hoboken, NJ: Wiley, 2010.

Williams, Kenneth. *Algebra for the Terrified*. Amazon Digital Services, 2013.

Wingard-Nelson, Rebecca. *Algebra and Pre-Algebra*. Berkeley Heights, NJ: Enslow Publishers, 2014.

Wingard-Nelson, Rebecca. *Algebra I and Algebra II Smarts!* Berkeley Heights, NJ: Enslow Publishers, 2011.

Wingard-Nelson, Rebecca. *Algebra Word Problems*. Berkeley Heights, NJ: Enslow Publishers, 2013.

Zaccaro, Edward. *Real World Algebra*. Bellevue, IA: Hickory Grove Press, 2001.

Index